ISBN 978-1-331-42628-8
PIBN 10188543

1 MONTH OF
FREE
READING

at
www.ForgottenBooks.com

By purchasing this book you are eligible for one month membership to ForgottenBooks.com, giving you unlimited access to our entire collection of over 700,000 titles via our web site and mobile apps.

To claim your free month visit:
www.forgottenbooks.com/free188543

English
Français
Deutsche
Italiano
Español
Português

www.forgottenbooks.com

Mythology Photography **Fiction**
Fishing Christianity **Art** Cooking
Essays Buddhism Freemasonry
Medicine **Biology** Music **Ancient
Egypt** Evolution Carpentry Physics
Dance Geology **Mathematics** Fitness
Shakespeare **Folklore** Yoga Marketing
Confidence Immortality Biographies
Poetry **Psychology** Witchcraft
Electronics Chemistry History **Law**
Accounting **Philosophy** Anthropology
Alchemy Drama Quantum Mechanics
Atheism Sexual Health **Ancient History**
Entrepreneurship Languages Sport
Paleontology Needlework Islam
Metaphysics Investment Archaeology
Parenting Statistics Criminology
Motivational

This volume contains 3 4
    items. Each one is
    inventories and
    cataloged separately.

CONTENTS

Department of Education

CITY AND COUNTY OF SAN FRANCISCO .

STATE OF CALIFORNIA

COURSE OF STUDY

IN

ARITHMETIC

FOR THE

DAY ELEMENTARY
SCHOOLS

July, 1918

Department of Education

CITY AND COUNTY OF SAN FRANCISCO
STATE OF CALIFORNIA

COURSE OF STUDY
IN
ARITHMETIC

FOR THE

DAY ELEMENTARY SCHOOLS

July, 1918

SHANNON-CONMY

PRESENTED BY THE OFFICE

of the

Superintendent of Schools

Authorized by the
Board of Education

FOR USE DURING THE SCHOOL YEAR 1918-19

Board of Education
GEORGE E. GALLAGHER, President
DR. A. A. D'ANCONA   SARAH J. JONES   AGNES G. REGAN

Superintendent of Schools
ALFRED RONCOVIERI

Deputy Superintendents of Schools
A. J. CLOUD   W. H. DE BELL   MARY MAGNER
R. H. WEBSTER

ACKNOWLEDGMENT

This Course of Study in Arithmetic was prepared and submitted by a First Committee of principals and teachers appointed by the Superintendent, was reviewed by a Second Committee similarly constituted and appointed, and has been given final revision by the Superintendent and staff of Deputy Superintendents. The Committees and the Deputy Superintendents have examined exhaustively a large number of the latest Courses of Study and a long list of standard texts. The Course is the outcome of this research based upon wide teaching experience.

The Superintendent takes this opportunity of expressing his sincere thanks to the many devoted workers who have participated in the formulation of this Course of Study, especially to those who have given so generously of their time and labor by serving on the Committees. The membership of these Committees was:

First Committee

Mrs. T. F. Spencer, Principal, Chairman
Mrs. M. M. FitzGerald, Principal
Mrs. A. F. Holden
Miss A. E. Casey
Miss Lillian Koch
Miss Retta H. Haynes
Miss Elizabeth Natusch

Second Committee

Miss E. G. Howard, Principal, Chairman
Miss I. R. Brown
Miss A. V. Casamayou
Miss M. Sayles
Miss M. S. Hall
Miss Nanno Livingston
Miss B. J. Klaus

ALFRED RONCOVIERI,
Superintendent of Schools.

San Francisco, California,
July, 1918.

ARITHMETIC

INTRODUCTION

PURPOSE.—This Course of Study has been planned with two distinct ends in mind. (1) To give the child a mastery of arithmetical facts and processes. (2) To give the child a knowledge of common business and other situations in which arithmetical combinations and manipulations are ordinarily used, so that he may understand them and reason from them with correctness.

CONTENT OF SUBJECT.—The list of topics required in arithmetic during the eight years of elementary school work is surprisingly small, and even this content is being diminished by the elimination of technical problems and applications that properly belong to schools of higher grade. Virtually, all that is required, or that it is practical to teach in the elementary school is a thorough knowledge of addition, subtraction, multiplication and division; of the fundamental processes in the manipulation of common and decimal fractions and of their applications; of simple percentage and its uses in ordinary business; of compound numbers not exceeding three denominations; and of the ratio of numbers.

A Course of Study then is merely designed to segregate these topics and to assign them to the different grades in the order best suited to the capacity of the pupil.

CHANGES FROM FORMER COURSE.—In preparing this Course of Study the following changes from the former Course have been made:

1. The Topical Method, in which a definite topic is assigned to each Grade as a year's work, has been substituted for the Spiral Method, in which subjects are taught recurrently from Grade to Grade.

2. Some subjects have been altogether eliminated, as Bank Discount, Duties, Negotiable Paper, etc., or greatly simplified, as Mensuration, Metric System, etc.

3. The work in all Primary Grades has been reorganized.

MINIMUM COURSE.—The Course herein outlined provides but the minimum of work. It should therefore be liberally supplemented by material from other sources.

DRILLS.—In each grade the time for *drill* should decrease, as the new work will utilize the *processes* of the preceding grades and will provide the necessary drill. *It is well to start the new work as soon as possible at the beginning of the term.* Too much time devoted to review of processes already mastered tends to dull the interest.

OBJECTIVE WORK.—Every new situation or process should be introduced concretely with much objective work. Objective work has its place just as much in the higher grades as in the lower. *Whenever a child is confused about the meaning of an arithmetical situation or the truth of a combination, an appeal to actual objects will aid his comprehension.*

BLACKBOARD AND SEAT WORK.—It is essential that children get correct impressions at the beginning. Hence, teachers in the earliest stages of teaching any given fact should have a large control over the work. The following typical stages are suggested: (1) The teacher performs the work at the blackboard, while the children merely observe. (2) The children do the work at the blackboard in plain sight of the teacher who supervises closely so as to catch errors quickly. (3) The children work at the seats with the teacher supervising. Work should be thoroughly developed, understood and memorized before this stage is reached. (4) Home-work: While arithmetic is the least desirable subject for homework, the best assignment of home-work in Arithmetic is the collecting of data on some given topic; *e. g.*, grocery store prices, prices of cotton goods, measuring and recording measurements of surfaces, estimating areas of neighborhood lots, etc.

NUMBER LANGUAGE.—School work in arithmetic does not always deal with real situations. It more frequently does not. It usually substitutes a *description* for the *situation*. When a child works with an arithmetic problem he is working with a description of the situation. Hence it is very important that the teacher develop a clear knowledge of such arithmetical terms as are used in arithmetical descriptions. The words add, subtract, or the signs $+$ or $-$ must stand for something definite in number, just as the words longitude and latitude and the signs N, S, E, and W do in geography. Children will not understand the situation they are dealing with unless they understand the language which describes it.

All problems are to be presented to the child *orally* up to the Fourth Grade. Pupils of the Third and Fourth Grades may use paper and pencil in performing the operation. Written problems are much more difficult for the child to understand, and should be given for the first time in the Fourth Grade, and, at first, in very simple language. The teacher should avoid giving problems the elements of which are buried in the previous problems of the same series. In order to test the pupil's understanding of a given situation the teacher should require him constantly to make and solve problems of a similar kind.

THE PRESENTATION OF ARITHMETICAL PROBLEMS.—Arithmetical problems or examples may be presented to the child in three ways: (1) The situation may present a problem, or (2) the problem may be presented orally, or (3) the problem may be presented in written or printed form.

At the beginning of any new line of work, the problem should be presented by the first method, *i. e.* objectively. After the situation is understood, oral presentation should be the main method. Not until the process or situation is well understood should there be a written presentation. No written presentation of problems is required before the fourth year, but the teacher may read problems to the child in any earlier grade.

The higher in the grades that arithmetic is taught the more important it becomes to understand the setting in which the arithmetical process is demanded. The main difficulty in the higher grades is to discover the steps to be performed, rather than in performing the steps. The main emphasis in the upper grades is on *reasoning* from the situation, which must be clearly understood. The main emphasis in the lower grades is on *memorizing the combinations. Both lines of work are always parallel, however.*

There will be days, therefore, in upper grade arithmetic on which business institutions will be studied without reference to any use of numbers or number processes, just as the institutions of government, or commerce, or transportation are treated in geography. Such work gives the child a better understanding of the situation in which he is to do his "figuring." It is important in business life to know both *what* to do and *how* to do it.

MENTAL, ORAL AND WRITTEN ARITHMETIC. — Strictly speaking *all arithmetic is mental.* But the mental processes may assume different forms of expression. The work may be done (a) silently, (b) orally, (c) in written fórm on paper or blackboard, or (d) by a mixture of any two or all three of these ways. The last or mixed method is the usual way in life. *All four of these ways of "doing" arithmetic should be used in the school throughout the grades from V to VIII.*

When numbers are small, work the examples without words, pencil or crayon. Every new step should be introduced with small numbers, and a large amount of work without pencil or crayon should be done.

Oral arithmetic and written arithmetic, wherein the statement, the process, and the result are completely expressed, are valuable mainly to let the teacher see just how the child has performed the operation. One of these methods is always essential in the attempt to discover why and where a child has failed to get the right answer or solution.

As there is no State Text devoted exclusively to mental (oral) arithmetic, teachers will make complete use of the oral work contained in the State Texts and are urged to supplement with some other standard text such as "Mental Arithmetic," Hopkins and Underwood.

Use of the Text-Book.—The *California State Series Elementary Arithmetic* is the text-book to be used, though it is to be in the *hands of the teacher only* during the first two years. During the Third, Fourth, and Fifth years the book should be in the hands of the pupil.

As the Text-Book has been compiled for a Spiral Course, and not for a Topical Course, it has been found necessary to specify certain pages. These are *guides* only. The teacher will use the examples on these pages suitable to the grade work, *omitting all others*. The State Text should be largely supplemented by "City Arithmetics," by Wentworth, Smith, Shiels, and other standard texts, and by Bulletin Number II of the San Francisco State Normal School.

Where a method is stated in the Course of Study it takes precedence over that in the State Text. Otherwise the Text-Book should be followed. In the development of the work, in all grades, each step in the Text-Book should be followed carefully.

Standardized Tests.—Standardized tests for measuring efficiency in the fundamental processes should be used. These tests save much time in determining the need for drill work and enable the teacher to estimate the relative strength of the pupil's work. Thompson's "Minimum Essentials" are of good practical value for drill.

PUPIL'S SELF-TESTING.—Self-reliance and the help of the teacher are both necessary to the child; they are not contradictions. Self-reliance must have a basis in a feeling of confidence and certainty in one's work. Hence, mental exercises and the checking and proving of results have their value. When the child has mastered the combinations in addition and multiplication (4-B Grade), it is well to give some practical check or test method by which *he can "measure up" his own work.* Yet self-reliance must grow out of the teacher's help. The teacher must lead the pupil to see the value of independent effort; yet must avoid the weakness of over-explanation. The teacher should avoid being a crutch for a pupil who is not lame; he needs to go slowly, that is all.

The following are simple applications of the old "casting out nines," and are to be used as self-tests by the pupils.

ADDITION

Adding horizontally,	628 =	16 =	7
" "	143 =	8 =	8
" "	769 =	22 =	4
" "	827 =	17 =	8

2367

$27 = 9$ ⎫
$ = 9$ ⎬ Check

Adding horizontally, 2367 = 18

MULTIPLICATION

$$\begin{array}{r} 4623 \\ \times 426 \\ \hline 27738 \\ 9246 \\ 18492 \\ \hline 1969398 \end{array}$$

Proof

Adding horizontally, as above in addition,

$4623 = 15 = 6$
$426 = 12 = 3$
$6 \times 3 = 18 = 9$ ⎫
Adding horizontally, $1969398 = 45 = 9$ ⎬ Check

DIVISION

$$193\,\overline{)68974}\quad 357\tfrac{73}{193}$$

Proof

Adding horizontally, as above in
addition,

$$193 = 13 = 4$$
$$357 = 15 = 6$$
$$73 = 10 = 1$$
$$4\times6+1 = 25 = 7$$

Adding horizontally,

$$68974 = 34 = 7$$

Check

REVIEWS.—It is not necessary to have many reviews. They should be used from time to time to determine the progress of pupils weak in particular parts of their work. Be sure to diagnose each individual case to determine whether failure results from deficient power to compute, from lack of knowledge of processes, from lack of drill, from inability to understand the conditions of a problem and the language in which it is stated, or from inability to reason from stated conditions.

Weekly or semi-monthly written tests are also unnecessary, as these tend to divert the pupil's interest from the *study of arithmetic* to the rating he receives on the tests. Thus, he loses sight of the *real* object of studying arithmetic.

BIBLIOGRAPHY

A Serviceable List for the Teacher

Watson & White..................................Elementary Arithmetic
Watson & White..................................Complete Arithmetic
Walsh, Suzzallo..................Arithmetic, Fundamental Processes
Walsh, Suzzallo..................Arithmetic, Practical Applications
Wentworth, Smith, Shiels........City Arithmetics, Grades 1 to 8
Hamilton's Standard Arithmetics:
    Book One,   First Four Grades.
    Book Two,   Fifth and Sixth Grades.
    Book Three, Seventh and Eighth Grades.
Byrnes, Richman, Roberts..
..................................The Pupils' Arithmetic, Books 1 to 6
Silver, Burdette..................................Arithmetics, Books 1 to 3
Hunt..Community Arithmetic
Wentworth and Smith..................Work and Play with Numbers
Smith, Eugene..................................The Teaching of Arithmetic
Brown and Coffman..................How to Teach Arithmetic
Robbins........Problems in Arithmetic (for 7th and 8th Grades)
Bogle..................................Everyday Bookkeeping
Farmer and Huntington..................................Food Problems
Chapin..................Model Store Demonstration Drills

For Optional Work in the Eighth Grade

Rowe..................................Junior Arithmetic Bookkeeping
Wentworth, Smith, Brown....Junior High School Mathematics

ARITHMETIC
GRADE 1-A
Definite Work—Counting
Time: Fifteen minutes' daily recitation.

ALL WORK ORAL

Reading of numbers.—To 30.

Counting.—With objects to 30.

Measuring.—No definite units. Measure by steps, handfuls, etc.

OUTLINE OF WORK

As the arithmetic of this Grade gives the child his first concept of number, the work should be simple and within his experience.

Counting is the foundation of all arithmetic. It should be done with and without objects. This is very necessary if the child is to get a correct idea of number.

Objects for counting should be varied, but color, size and material should be uniform; spools, splints, cubes, buttons, etc., are suggested.

Let the work be live and interesting; avoid mechanical lessons. Let all knowledge come through motor activity. Let the children count everything possible in the room—desks, windows, etc. Let them count objects to each other, steps across the room, steps around the room, etc.

All arithmetic in this Grade is to be subordinated to the more important needs of language. Number work is really language work by which children are trained to *hear* and interpret simple directions. Teachers must allow sufficient time for all pupils to interpret the direction and to image its execution.

Observe most minutely all directions in Paragraph 1, Lesson 1, Text-Book.

As far as possible, make the exercise in number stories in a single class-exercise deal with one set of topics, such as "a grocery store," "a bakery shop," etc. This will make the stories real to the child and prevent the disconnected work which scatters the child's attention over many things during one lesson.

TEXT-BOOK. California State Series. Elementary Arithmetic, pages 7 to 17, inclusive—in hands of teacher only.

RECOMMENDED FOR SUPPLEMENTARY WORK. City Arithmetics, Grade I (Wentworth, Smith, Shiels).

GRADE 1-B

Definite Work—Geometric Form and Magnitude

Time: Twenty minutes' daily recitation.

ORAL

Reading of numbers.—To 100. Number table, page 17, Text-Book.

Counting.—By tens, beginning at 1, as 1, 11, 21
" " " " 2, " 2, 12, 22
" " . " " 3, " 3, 13, 23

(Pages 12 and 13, Text-Book.)

Direction.—"In right hand," etc., page 9, Text-Book.

Measurements.—Pages 7, 8, 9, Text-Book.

WRITTEN

(Emphasize the necessity of making neat, legible figures.)

Writing of numbers at blackboard.—To 100 (under direction of the teacher).

OUTLINE OF WORK

Plan work so as to furnish constant opportunities for the exercise of powers of comparison and judgment.

Use *real measures:* yard stick, foot rule, pint and quart measures.

Follow plans of Lessons 7 and 8, Text-Book.

All work should be concrete. Develop the idea of form, as shown in Lesson 9, Text-Book. Use comparison of lines, surfaces and solids to develop the idea of *longer than, shorter than,* etc. No exact ratio is required; the thought of *magnitude* is to be realized.

Teach "zero" for 0.

Teach the names of the months and the days of the week.

Use number stories to illustrate the work of this grade. As far as possible have such stories in a single day's work deal with one set of topics, as "a fruit store," or "the schoolroom."

TEXT-BOOK. California State Series, Elementary Arithmetic, Chapter 2—in hands of teacher only.

RECOMMENDED FOR SUPPLEMENTARY WORK. City Arithmetics, Grade I (Wentworth, Smith, Shiels). Busy Builders, Cobb.

GRADE 2-A

Definite Work—Preparation for Addition and Subtraction

Time: Twenty-five minutes' daily recitation—two-thirds oral, one-third written.

ORAL

Reading of numbers.—To 1000.

Counting.—By two's beginning with 2, by three's beginning with 3, etc., to 50.

Drill.—Pages 48 and 49 (through Lesson 12), Text-Book.

Measurement.—Inch, foot, pint, quart, dozen. U. S. money: 5 cents, 10 cents (dime), 25 cents (quarter dollar), 50 cents (half dollar), dollar.

WRITTEN

(Emphasize the necessity of making neat, legible figures.)

Writing of numbers.—To 1000.

Rapid Drill Exercises.—Page 19, Text-Book.

OUTLINE OF WORK

Begin with bundles of tens, using splints, cards, etc.

Then count by tens, using number-table, page 17, Text-Book.

Develop and *impress* the fact that the units' figure does not change, no matter what prefix is used as the tens' figure.

Study steps A and B, as given in Chapter 2, pages 34 and 35, Text-Book.

Develop concretely the combinations in Lesson A, page 47, Text-Book.

Have pupils use number-cards made by themselves under teacher's direction. Memorize the combinations (Study-Exercises, page 48), after they are developed.

Teach combinations with 0 and 1.

Use number stories and *oral* problems as suggested on page 47, Text-Book. As far as possible make the day's problems deal with a single topic.

Develop the ideas of *more* and *less,* of *making greater* and *making less.* Similarly, study and develop subtraction combinations, Lesson A, page 51, Text-Book, but teach by *taking away.* Thus, the first exercise on the right in Lesson A is read 6 *from* 10 leaves how many?

There is *no formal* addition or subtraction in this grade. The work is preparatory only. It should be made very interesting by giving, lending, playing store and using toy money.

Review work of preceding grade.

TEXT-BOOK. California State Series, Elementary Arithmetic, Chapters 2 and 3, specified pages—in hands of teacher only.

RECOMMENDED FOR SUPPLEMENTARY WORK. City Arithmetics, Grade II (Wentworth, Smith, Shiels).

GRADE 2-B

Definite Work—Addition and Subtraction

Time: Twenty-five minutes' daily recitation—two-thirds oral, one-third written.

ORAL

Reading of numbers.—To 10,000. Roman numerals to XII.

Addition.—Combinations on page 47, Text-Book.

Subtraction.—Combinations on page 51, Text-Book.

Drill—Follow steps A and B, page 48, Text-Book.

Measurement.—Review measures taught in preceding grades. Teach gallon, yard, and telling time.

Problems.—Daily, applying combinations as above, in work suited to the Grade.

WRITTEN

(Emphasize the necessity of making neat, legible figures.)

Writing of numbers.—To 10,000.

Combinations.—As
$$4 \qquad 4 \qquad 4$$
$$+5 \quad +15 \quad +25 \text{ etc.,}$$

$$3 \qquad 3 \qquad 3$$
$$+2 \quad +12 \quad +22 \text{ etc., through all five}$$
combinations of Lesson A, and combinations with 0 and 1.

Use number-cards made as directed in Grade 2-A.

There is no borrowing nor carrying in subtraction.

Teach plus (+) and minus (—) signs; sum and difference.

OUTLINE OF WORK

Review rapidly the *foundation* work given in Grade 2-A. When steps A and B, pages 34 and 35, Text-Book, have been reviewed, give step C as presented on pages 36 and 49, Text-Book. Then begin on column 1, lesson 13, page 49.

Always begin with oral drill of all combinations in each exercise. Do not be in a hurry; *do not call the combinations for the pupil.*

	4		4 ⌐ 19		15	and	4	are	19
When he has	3		3 ⌐ 15		5	"	4	"	9
mastered:	2	give	12	as follows:	12	"	3	"	15
					2	"	3	"	5

Then erase the helping figures 15 and 19. Let the *child* begin 12, 15. If he cannot, let *him* call the combinations himself, as "2 and 3 are 5," "12 and 3 are 15," until he learns them.

San Francisco State Normal Bulletin, No. 11, gives excellent drill sets on these combinations.

Teach Subtraction by "taking away."

Teach the correct form "two hundred one, three hundred one, three hundred four," not "two hundred *and* one, three hundred *and* four," etc.

TEXT-BOOK. California State Series, Elementary Arithmetic, pages 48 to 56, inc., omitting page 50—in hands of teacher only.

RECOMMENDED FOR SUPPLEMENTARY WORK. City Arithmetics, Grade II (Wentworth, Smith, Shiels). San Francisco State Normal Bulletin, No. 11.

GRADE 3-A

Definite Work—Addition, Subtraction, U. S. Money

Time: Thirty minutes' daily recitation—one-half oral, one-half written.

ORAL

Reading of numbers.—To 100,000. Roman numerals to L.

Combinations.—Pages 57, 59, 65, and 67, Text-Book.

Problems.—Daily, applying combinations as above, in work suited to the Grade.

Measurement.—Review yard, foot, inch; pint, quart and gallon.

Signs and Terms.—Plus (+), minus (—); sum and difference.

WRITTEN

(Emphasize the necessity of making neat, legible figures.)

Writing of numbers.—To 100,000.

Addition.—No addition at seats. Examples dictated for board work.

Subtraction.—Teach carrying—"taking away" method, as follows:

```
  246        8 from 16 leaves 8
 — 58        6  "    14   "   8
 ——          1  "     2   "   1
  188
```

Continue use of number-cards, as in Grade 2-A.

OUTLINE OF WORK

In teaching U. S. money do not speak of the decimal point as such. Explain it as a necessary dividing mark between dollars and cents.

In this Grade for the first time the Text-Book is placed in the hands of the pupils. Let the children *read* the problems on pages 57, 59, 61, 62, 63, etc., so as to bring out the *meaning* clearly, before attempting to solve them.

Teach the pupils to see that problems merely use the facts already learned about number relations. *Encourage them to give examples of their own.* Open a store, let them buy and sell, using the numbers they know. Make the work live and interesting.

From such a statement as $\frac{139}{-93}$ let the children frequently give and solve concrete problems.

TEXT-BOOK. California State Series, Elementary Arithmetic, pages 57 to 71, omitting page 64—in the hands of the children.

RECOMMENDED FOR SUPPLEMENTARY USE. City Arithmetics, Grade III (Wentworth, Smith, Shiels). Model Store Demonstration Drills (Chapin).

GRADE 3-B

Definite Work—Multiplication Tables

Time: Thirty minutes' daily recitation—one-half oral, one-half written.

ORAL

Reading of numbers.—To 1,000,000. Roman Numerals to C.

Combinations—Lessons D, E, F, pages 73 to 95, inclusive, Text-Book (excluding multiplication, division, and fractions).

Tables.—Through 9 times 12.

Problems.—Daily, applying combinations as above in work suited to the Grade.

Measurements.—Minute, hour, day, week, month, year. Review measures previously studied.

WRITTEN

(Emphasize the necessity of making neat, legible figures.)

Writing of numbers.—Through 1,000,000.

Addition and subtraction.—Pages 73 to 95, inclusive, Text-Book. Drill for accuracy. Review preceding combinations.

Continue use of number-cards as directed in Grade 2-A.

OUTLINE OF WORK

Continue to develop and teach addition and subtraction combinations as outlined in the Text-Book. As soon as formal work is mastered, it should be applied in problem form. Emphasize the *reading* of the written problems and the *making* of original problems.

Have pupils *memorize* the multiplication tables. *Do not apply them.*

PUPILS SHOULD MAKE THEIR OWN TABLE-CARDS AND USE THEM IN SILENT STUDY.

Model store work is excellent for this grade.

TEXT-BOOK. California State Series, Elementary Arithmetic.

RECOMMENDED FOR SUPPLEMENTARY USE. City Arithmetics, Grade III (Wentworth. Smith, Shiels). Model Store Demonstration Drills (Chapin). San Francisco State Normal Bulletin, No. 11.

GRADE 4-A

Definite Work—Multiplication and Short Division

Time: Thirty minutes' daily recitation—one-half oral, one-half written.

ORAL

Reading of numbers.—To 10,000,000. Roman Numerals, review and extend, and note their application.

Combinations.—Lessons G and H, pages 97 to 111, inclusive, Text-Book (omitting page 104).

Tables.—As far as 12 times 12.

Measurement.—Ounce, pound, ton.

Problems.—Daily, applying combinations as above, in work suited to the Grade.

Terms and Signs.—Product and Quotient and signs " $\times$ " and " $\div$ ".

WRITTEN

(Emphasize the necessity of making neat, legible figures.)

Writing of numbers.—To 10,000,000.

Addition and subtraction.—Application of Lessons G and H. Frequent review of combinations previously studied.

Multiplication.—Apply tables—first one figure, then two.

Division.—Short division through nine.

OUTLINE OF WORK

In this grade the combinations in addition and subtraction should be completed. Work for speed and accuracy in these subjects. As the multiplication tables have been memorized in Grade 3-B, their application should not be difficult.

Use cards in reviewing tables.

Have mental arithmetic daily, using the number combinations which have been studied.

As soon as formal work is mastered. it should be applied in problem form. Emphasize the *reading* of written problems and the *making* of original problems.

Socialize the work. Use model store, if possible.

TEXT-BOOK. California State Series, Elementary Arithmetic.

RECOMMENDED FOR SUPPLEMENTARY WORK. City Arithmetics, Grade IV (Wentworth, Smith, Shiels). Model Store Demonstration Drills (Chapin). San Francisco State Normal Bulletin, No. 11.

GRADE 4-B

Definite Work—Long Division

Time: Thirty minutes' daily recitation—one-half oral, one-half written.

ORAL

Reading of numbers.—To 100,000,000.

Addition.—All combinations.

Subtraction.—All combinations.

Multiplication.—Application of tables through 12 times 12.

Problems.—Daily, applying combinations as above, in work suited to the Grade.

Measurements.—Square inch, square foot, square yard.

. WRITTEN

(Emphasize the necessity of making neat, legible figures.)

Writing of numbers.—To 100,000,000. Dollars and cents.

Addition and subtraction.—Work for rapidity and accuracy.

Multiplication.—Multiplication of not more than six figures in the multiplicand nor three in the multiplier; zero difficulty.

Division.—Review short division. Teach long division.

Application of multiplication.—Bill forms as on page 177, Text-Book.

Use checking method as given in the Introduction to this Course.

OUTLINE OF WORK

Review work studied in Chapter 4, Text-Book. Use a horizontal line to express division, as on page 135. It makes a brief statement possible.

Since Short Division has been previously taught, Long Division should give little trouble. Disregard the treatment of the subject on pages 178-185 of the Text-Book.

Place on the blackboard a copy of the accompanying diagram, showing the four steps in the process of Long Division. By this device the pupil can see at a glance each step in the recurring cycles.

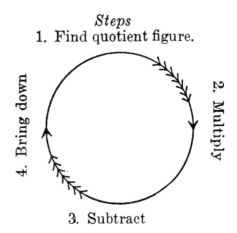

Steps
1. Find quotient figure.

2. Multiply

4. Bring down

3. Subtract

The first of these steps—finding the quotient figure—is the only one that offers any real difficulty. But this step becomes very easy and readily automatic if the pupil is taught the *language* and *method* of the following illustrative example:

FINDING QUOTIENT FIGURE

Step 1

a. How many 4's in 22?

b. There are 5, and 2 over, making my next number 27.

c. But are there 5 3's in 27?

d. Yes. Then 5 is my quotient figure.

(Then multiply, subtract, bring down, making new dividend 125.)

```
           52
43 )2275
       215
      ----
       125
        86
      ----
        39
```

a. How many 4's in 12?

b. There are 3 and 0 over, making my next number 5.

c. But are there 3 3's in 5?

d. No. Then 2 is my quotient figure.

(Again multiply, subtract, etc.)

When Long Division has been thoroughly mastered, according to the above method, indicate to the pupil a shorter method of testing, as, for example, with the divisor 18 or 19, 2 may be used as the trial divisor; or, with the divisor 91 or 92, 9 may be so used.

No fractions are introduced in this Grade.

Have the work socialized: thus, have the pupils bring in bill heads, and make real bills.

As soon as formal work is mastered, it should be applied in problem form.

The first problems should always involve figures that can be worked "mentally." Begin analysis of simple problems, one-step only. Have pupils *read* problems to get an understanding of what is required, what is given, etc.

Upon completing Grade 4-B work, pupils should:

(1) Have mastered the four fundamental operations;
(2) Be accurate and rapid in operations;
(3) Make neat and legible numbers; and,
(4) Be able to reason out and work simple problems.

TEXT-BOOK. California State Series, Elementary Arithmetic.

RECOMMENDED FOR SUPPLEMENTARY WORK. City Arithmetics, Grade IV (Wentworth, Smith, Shiels). Model Store Demonstration Drills (Chapin). San Francisco State Normal Bulletin, No. 11.

GRADE 5-A

Definite Work—Fractions, Addition and Subtraction

Time: Thirty-five minutes' daily recitation—one-fourth oral; three-fourths written.

ORAL

Addition ⎫ Begin each day's work with rapid number
Subtraction ⎪ drill to secure power in the use of the
Multiplication ⎬ combinations. This work must supple-
Division ⎭ ment the written work.

Problems.—Daily, applying subject-matter in work suited to the Grade.

Fractions.—Teach numerator, denominator, different kinds of fractions, and common denominator.

Measurements.—Review tables of preceding Grades.

WRITTEN

(Emphasize the necessity of making neat, legible figures.)

Review.—Writing numbers through 100,000,000. All fundamental operations. Drill for accuracy first.

Fractions.—Addition, subtraction, reduction to lowest terms, mixed numbers, proper and improper fractions, as in Chapter 5, pages 188 to 205, Text-Book.

U. S. money.

Bills.—Simple accounts of four or five items to apply fundamentals.

Problems.—Simple one-step problems, as on pages 190 to 191, Text-Book.

OUTLINE OF WORK

Teach common denominator both by inspection and factoring. Use no higher denominator than twenty.

As soon as formal work is mastered, it should be applied in problem form. Make all problem work simple and concrete, applying as far as possible to every day experiences.

TEXT-BOOK. California State Series, Elementary Arithmetic.

RECOMMENDED FOR SUPPLEMENTARY WORK. City Arithmetics, Grade V (Wentworth, Smith, Shiels). Mental Arithmetic (Hopkins and Underwood). San Francisco Normal Bulletin, No. 11. Model Store Demonstration Drills (Chapin).

GRADE 5-B

Definite Work—Fractions, Multiplication and Division

Time: Thirty-five minutes' daily recitation—one-fourth oral, three-fourths written.

ORAL

Daily drill.—Aim at thought and accuracy. Use simple numbers preparatory to written work.

Review all terms used in fractional work.

Problems.—Daily, applying subject-matter in work suited to the Grade.

Measurements.—Review tables of preceding Grades.

WRITTEN

(Emphasize the necessity of making neat, legible figures.)

Review writing of numbers.—Through 100,000,000.

Fundamentals.—Daily review. Work for accuracy first, then speed.

Fractions.—Cover Text-Book, pages 206 to 226.

U. S. money.—Aliquot parts of a dollar applied in household accounts.

OUTLINE OF WORK

Teach cancellation, and its application, using small numbers. Make household accounts, using fractional multipliers, giving preference to those usually found in business.

As soon as formal work is mastered, it should be applied in problem form. Pupils should use problems on cards for busy work at blackboard. Continue work in a model store. Use *real* bill heads; make the work *real*.

Treat pages 224 and 225, Text-Book, as simple analysis.

TEXT-BOOK. California State Series, Elementary Arithmetic.

RECOMMENDED FOR SUPPLEMENTARY WORK. City Arithmetics, Grade V (Wentworth, Smith, Shiels). Mental Arithmetic (Hopkins and Underwood). San Francisco State Normal Bulletin No. 11. Model Store Demonstration Drills (Chapin).

GRADE 6-A
Definite Work—Decimals

Time: Thirty-five minutes' daily recitation—one-fourth oral, three-fourths written.

ORAL

Daily drill.—Aim at thought and accuracy. Use simple numbers preparatory to written work.

Problems.—Daily, applying subject-matter in work suited to the Grade.

WRITTEN

(Emphasize the necessity of making neat, legible figures.)

Whole numbers.—Review fundamental operations, to secure accuracy first, then speed.

Fractions.—Review addition, subtraction, multiplication and division, using simple, ordinary fractions.

Decimals.—Write from dictation through the six orders. Note relation of orders of decimals and of integers. Drill on the effect of moving the decimal point. Addition, subtraction, multiplication and division. Reduction of fractions to decimals and of decimals to fractions.

(California State Series, Elementary Arithmetic, in hands of teacher, pages 229-236.)

Problems.—Two-step reasoning. Analysis of simple problems.

Measurement.—Dry measure, liquid measure, avoirdupois. Prime factors.

OUTLINE OF WORK

California State Series, Advanced Arithmetic, in the hands of the pupils, pp. 15, 18, 19, 20, 25, 28 (follow carefully the plan given for solving problems), 31, 36, 37, 38, 39, 40, 41, 42, 43, 45, 68, 69, 70, 71, 72, 73, 76, 77, 87, 88, and 89.

As soon as formal work is mastered, it should be applied in problem form.

Socialize the work by using *real* situations, cash slips, cash accounts, etc.

TEXT-BOOK. California State Series, Advanced Arithmetic.

RECOMMENDED FOR SUPPLEMENTARY WORK. City Arithmetics, Grade VI (Wentworth, Smith, Shiels). Mental Arithmetic (Hopkins and Underwood). San Francisco State Normal Bulletin, No. 11, part 2. Food Problems (Farmer and Huntington).

GRADE 6-B

Definite Work—Measurements

Time: Thirty-five minutes' daily recitation—one-fourth oral, three-fourths written.

ORAL

Daily drill.—Aim at thought and accuracy. Use simple numbers preparatory to written work.

Problems.—Daily, applying subject-matter in work suited to the Grade.

WRITTEN

(Emphasize the necessity of making neat, legible figures.)

Whole Numbers.—Review fundamental operations to secure accuracy first, then speed.

Fractions.—Review addition, subtraction, multiplication and division.

Decimals.—Review the work given in the previous Grade.

Review reduction of fractions to decimals and decimals to fractions.

Measurement.—Square measure, cubic measure, linear measure, and time table.

Bills.—Business forms of all kinds.

Short methods.—Pages 148 and 149, Text-Book.

OUTLINE OF WORK

Teach square measure and cubic measure concretely. Use real and ordinary situations, such as paving streets, excavations, etc.. Use material from pages 72, 73, 76, 77, 78, and 80 to 86, Text-Book.

Drill on factoring and cancellation.

As soon as formal work is mastered, it should be applied in problem form.

TEXT-BOOK. California State Series, Advanced Arithmetic.

RECOMMENDED FOR SUPPLEMENTARY USE. City Arithmetics, Grade VI (Wentworth, Smith, Shiels). Mental Arithmetic (Hopkins and Underwood). San Francisco State Normal Bulletin, No. 11, part 2. Food Problems (Farmer and Huntington).

GRADE 7-A

Definite Work—Presentation of Percentage

Time: Forty minutes.

Time: Forty minutes' daily recitation—one-fourth oral, three-fourths written.

ORAL

Daily drill.—Aim at thought and accuracy. Use simple numbers preparatory to written work.

Problems.—Daily, applying subject-matter in work suited to the Grade.

WRITTEN

(Emphasize the necessity of making neat, legible figures.)

Fundamental Operations ⎫
Whole Numbers ⎪
Fractions ⎬ Review daily, first for accuracy,
Denominate Numbers ⎪ then for speed.
Decimals ⎭

Percentage.—-Teach percentage as a development of two place decimals, as $\frac{5}{100} = .05 = 5\%$.

Formal percentage, particularly the following four processes, in simple, concrete situations:

1. To find any per cent of a number.
2. To find what per cent one number is of another.
3. To find a number when a certain per cent of it is given.
4. To change any per cent to decimals or common fractions, or the reverse.

Bills.—Calculate in groups, as a dozen, a hundred, etc.

OUTLINE OF WORK

It is a very easy step from common fractions, or decimals, to percentage: $\frac{5}{100}$, or .05, or 5% (Text-Book, page 166).

Lesson 11, page 170, Text-Book, should be thoroughly memorized, so that the mention of the fraction automatically suggests the decimal equivalent. Present percentage in its relation to decimals and common fractions, showing how to change from one to the other readily.

In drilling upon the four formal processes of percentage above mentioned, use the shortest methods.

Pages 170 and 171, Text-Book, contain good oral exercises. Extend this work. Drill on such problems as, "If three dozen tablets cost 12 cents, how many dozen may be bought for 36 cents?" (To get the *group* idea.) As soon as formal work is mastered, it should be applied in problem form.

TEXT-BOOK. California State Series, Advanced Arithmetic.

RECOMMENDED FOR SUPPLEMENTARY WORK. City Arithmetics, Grade VII (Wentworth, Smith, Shiels). Mental Arithmetic (Hopkins and Underwood). Food Problems (Farmer and Huntington).

GRADE 7-B

Definite Work—Application of Percentage

Time: Forty minutes' daily recitation—one-fourth oral, three-fourths written.

ORAL

Daily drill.—Aim at thought and accuracy. Use simple numbers preparatory to written work.

Problems.—Daily, applying subject-matter in work suited to the Grade.

WRITTEN

(Emphasize the necessity of making neat, legible figures.)

Fractions }
Decimals } Review daily, first for accuracy, then for speed.

Percentage.—Teach its application to ordinary business transactions by showing the pupils that gain and loss, commission, insurance, taxes, trade discount, etc., are only variations of the same subject. (Text-Book, pages 181 to 205.)

OUTLINE OF WORK

Make the work as simple as possible. Give problems embodying situations with which the pupil is familiar. The reasons for trade discount, the underlying principle in insurance, the reasons for taxes, etc., should be made clear. Use city taxation: "How are cities taxed?" "Why are they taxed?" etc. This correlates well with Civics and Composition.

Continue to socialize the work. Discuss the nature and function of these various business relations, thus giving the pupils information just as valuable as the mere arithmetic, and making the work seem more real and useful to them.

TEXT-BOOK. California State Series, Advanced Arithmetic.

RECOMMENDED FOR SUPPLEMENTARY WORK. City Arithmetics, Grade VII (Wentworth, Smith, Shiels). Mental Arithmetic (Hopkins and Underwood). Food Problems (Farmer and Huntington).

GRADE 8-A

Definite Work—Interest and Ratio and Proportion

Time: Forty minutes' daily recitation—one-fourth oral, three-fourths written. .

ORAL

Daily drill.—Aim at thought and accuracy. Use simple numbers preparatory to written work.

Problems.—Daily, applying subject-matter in work suited to the Grade.

WRITTEN

(Emphasize the necessity of making neat, legible figures.)

Fractions } Review daily, first for accuracy, then for speed.
Decimals }

Interest.—Teach particularly the sixty days 6% method, page 212, Text-Book.

Ratio.—Develop the idea.

Proportion.—Teach that it is only the equality of ratios.

Business forms.—Money orders, checks, receipts, bills, etc.

OUTLINE OF WORK

The simplest way of computing interest is the sixty days 6% method. It affords much material for rapid mental work. Teach interest by this method only.

Illustration of Method

Any sum of money will double itself in 200 months or 6000 days at 6%:

Interest on $1250 for 200 mos. at 6% is $1250
"   "   1250 "   2 " " 6% "   12.50
"   "   1250 "   1 " " 6% "   6.25

Interest on $1250 for 6000 days at 6% is $1250
"   "   1250 "   600 "   " 6% "   125
"   "   1250 "   60 "   " 6% "   12.50
"   "   1250 "   6 "   " 6% "   1.25

The key to rapid and accurate work in the calculation of interest consists in the ability to find the exact number of days between two dates (time less than one year) and to apply the time most directly by some rule for finding interest.

Note well that the 6% method assumes the 360 day year, now common in business calculations, *e. g.* in the preparation of interest tables, etc. Practically, EXACT INTEREST (365 days to the year) is not paid any longer, except by the government. The 360 day year has replaced the 365 day year. Another change in business methods needs to be noted by the teacher—interest is now charged for every day the note runs. EXACT TIME is used in all calculations of financial institutions. It *cannot be found by compound subtraction.* The exact time is found by COUNTING the days from one date to another, or by employing tables for the purpose. (Use table and exercises, Text-Book, pages 267 and 268.)

Form:

Exact time from January 1, 1898, to July 7, 1899, is found thus:

Jan. 1, 1898, to Jan. 1, 1899—1 yr.

Jan.—	30	days.
Feb.—	28	"
Mar.—	31	"
Apr.—	30	"
May—	31	"
Jun.—	30	"
Jul.—	7	"

187 days.

Very rarely the time involved in a business paper is more than one year. When such is the case find the number of years and the exact days for the remainder of the time.

e. g.—Sept. 25, 1909 to June 24, 1911.

To Sept. 25, 1910, 1 year; from Sept. 25, 1910, to June 24, 1911 = 272 days.

Derived Problems or Indirect Cases of Interest.—After the principle of computing Interest is mastered, pupils may be taught the following simple plan for solving ''derived'' problems or problems in ''indirect cases'' of Interest:

With the form P $\times$ R $\times$ T $=$ I before them, let the pupils read the problem carefully, and place under each letter the quantity corresponding to the term, using a ? for the missing term; then proceed to work the equation.

Time must *always* be expressed in years or fractions of a year when the rate per cent is given by the year.

Use 360 days as the unit.

Teach Ratio as on pages 54, 91, 145, and 243, and Proportion as on page 243, Text-Book.

TEXT-BOOK. California State Series, Advanced Arithmetic.

RECOMMENDED FOR SUPPLEMENTARY WORK. City Arithmetics, Grade VIII (Wentworth, Smith, Shiels). Mental Arithmetic (Hopkins and Underwood). Food Problems (Farmer and Huntington).

GRADE 8-B

Definite Work—Measurements; Review

Time: Forty minutes' daily recitation, one-fourth oral, three-fourths written.

ORAL

Daily drill.—Aim at thought and accuracy. Use simple numbers preparatory to written work.

Problems.—Daily, applying subject-matter in work suited to the Grade.

WRITTEN

(Emphasize the necessity of making neat, legible figures.)

Squares and square roots.—Simple applications of square root.

Simple measurements.—Of surfaces, capacity of rooms, etc.

Review.—Common and decimal fractions, percentage, applications of percentage, simple interest.

Teach the writing and use of receipts and checks.

Teach uses of money orders and notes.

Drill on bills, and on cash, personal and household accounts.

Investing money.—Stocks and Bonds (Make the work concrete). (Time five days.) Explain the various technical terms of corporate business, pages 256 to 262, Text-Book. Explain stock quotations as given in daily papers. Distinguish between reliable and non-reliable bonds. Correlate with Civics. (Time ten days.)

Teach the tables of the Metric System, the prefixes and the units of the system and their English equivalents, pages 304 to 312, Text-Book. (Time fifteen days.)

Teach reading of gas meter, page 75, Text-Book.

Teach equations, pages 283 to 292, Text-Book.

OUTLINE OF WORK

Squares and square root.—Pages 244 to 249, Text-Book. Find roots by factoring when possible. Make the work very simple. In reviewing taxes, insurance, gain and loss, show the underlying principles. Make the lessons part of the Civics work. Show how the insurance companies can pay heavy losses on small premiums. Discuss taxable value of property, how taxes are apportioned, etc. Pupils should understand the different channels into which the city's revenues go.

Household and personal accounts are important. Short methods of computation should be used.

Note practical uses of Metric System.

TEXT-BOOK. California State Series, Advanced Arithmetic.

RECOMMENDED FOR SUPPLEMENTARY WORK. City Arithmetics, Grade VIII (Wentworth, Smith, Shiels). Mental Arithmetic (Hopkins and Underwood). Food Problems (Farmer and Huntington). Everyday Bookkeeping (Bogle). Community Arithmetic (Hunt). Junior Arithmetic Bookkeeping (Rowe).

CPSIA information can be obtained
at www.ICGtesting.com
Printed in the USA
BVHW041933291118
534359BV00013B/298/P